SCHIRMER'S LIBRARY
OF MUSICAL CLASSICS

Vol. 792

J. PISCHNA

Technical Studies

Sixty Progressive Exercises, Containing
Studies on Trills, Scales, Chords,
Passages and Arpeggios

For the Piano

Newly Revised and Augmented Edition
with Additional Preliminary Exercises by

BERNARD WOLFF

Translated from the German by
DR. THEODORE BAKER

G. SCHIRMER, Inc.

DISTRIBUTED BY

HAL•LEONARD®
CORPORATION

7777 W. BLUEMOUND RD. P.O. BOX 13819 MILWAUKEE, WI 53213

Preparatory Exercises to Nº 1ª

Practise in all keys.

J. Pischna.

Lento.

1ᵃ

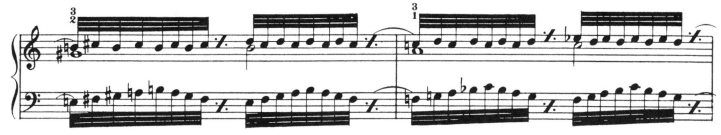

Preparatory Exercises to № 2ª

Practise in all keys.

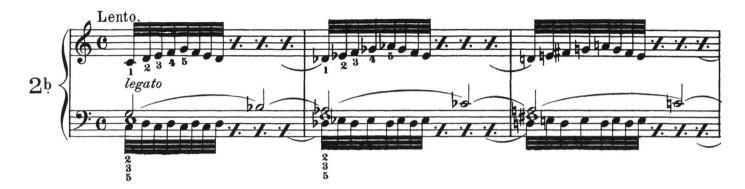

Preparatory Exercises to N⁰ 3.

Practise in all keys.

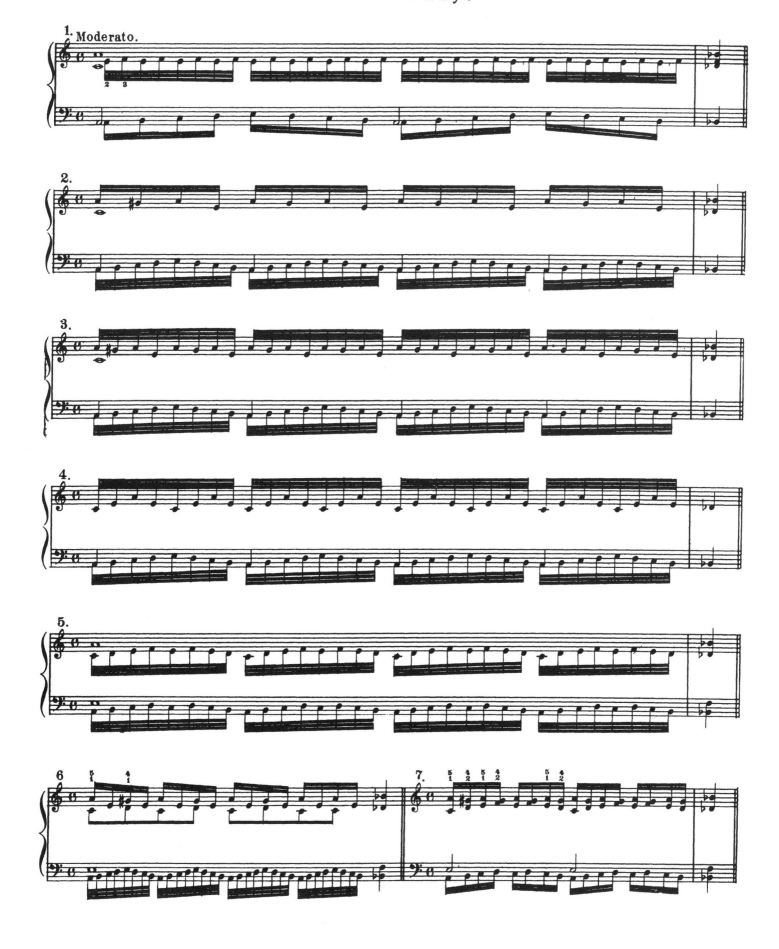

3.

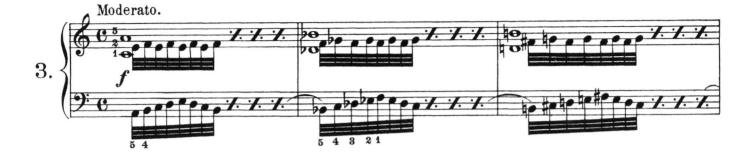

Preparatory Exercises to No. 4.

Practise in all keys.

Preparatory Exercises to № 5.

Practise in all keys.

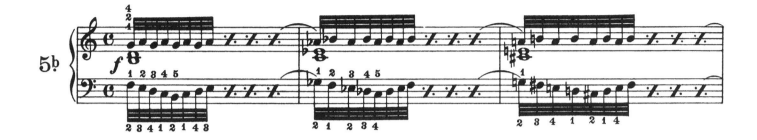

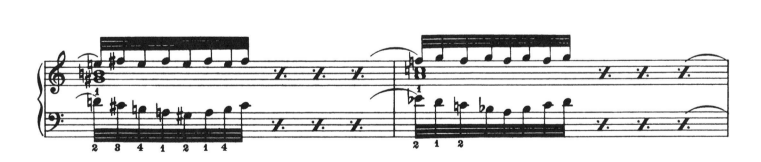

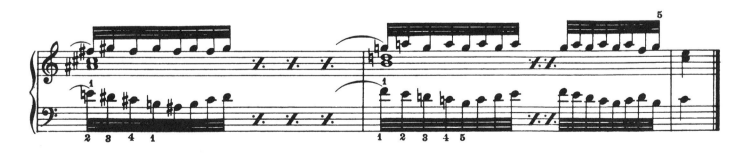

Preparatory Exercises to № 6.

Practise in all keys.

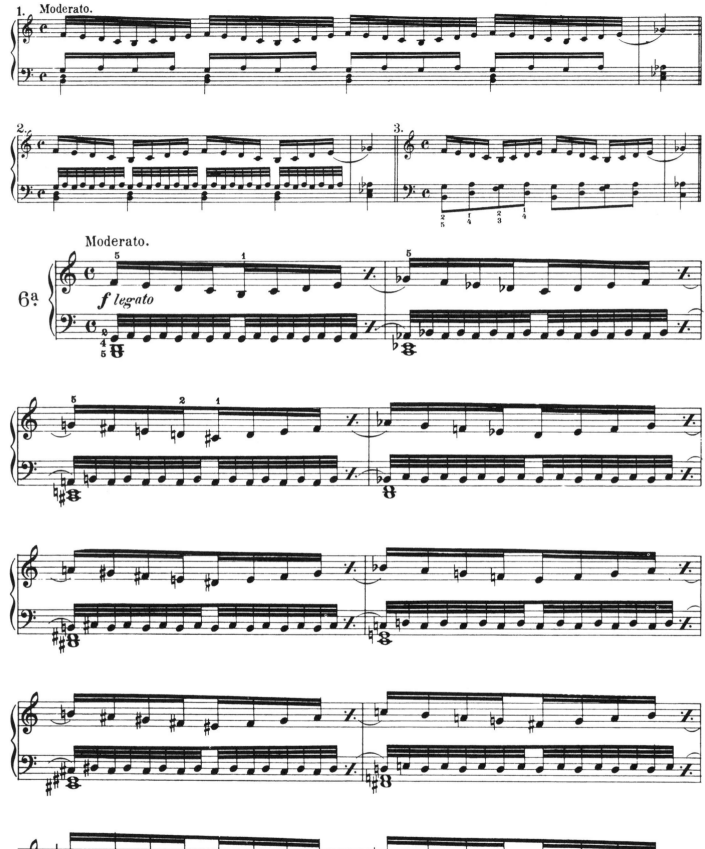

Preparatory Exercises to № 7.

Practise in all keys.

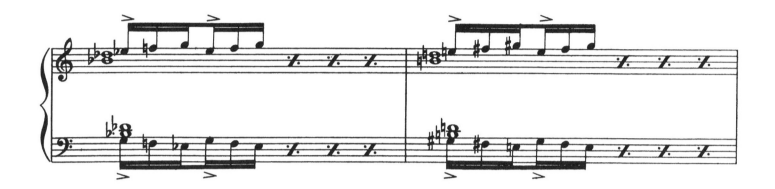

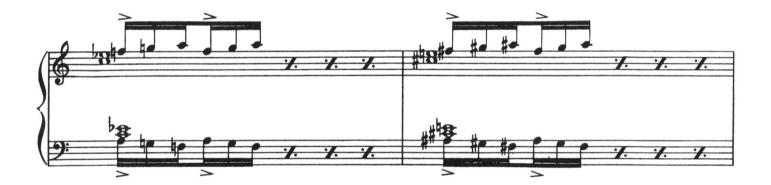

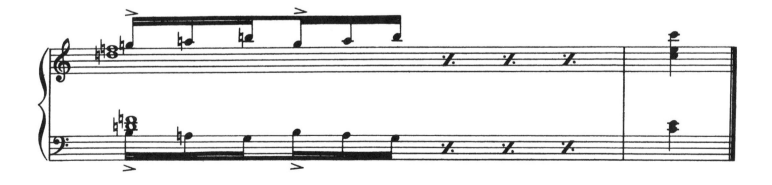

Preparatory Exercises to Nº 8.

Practise in all keys.

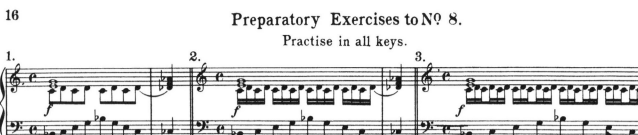

Hold down all the fingers.

Lento.

Hold down all the fingers.

Preparatory Exercises to Nº 9.

Practise in all keys.

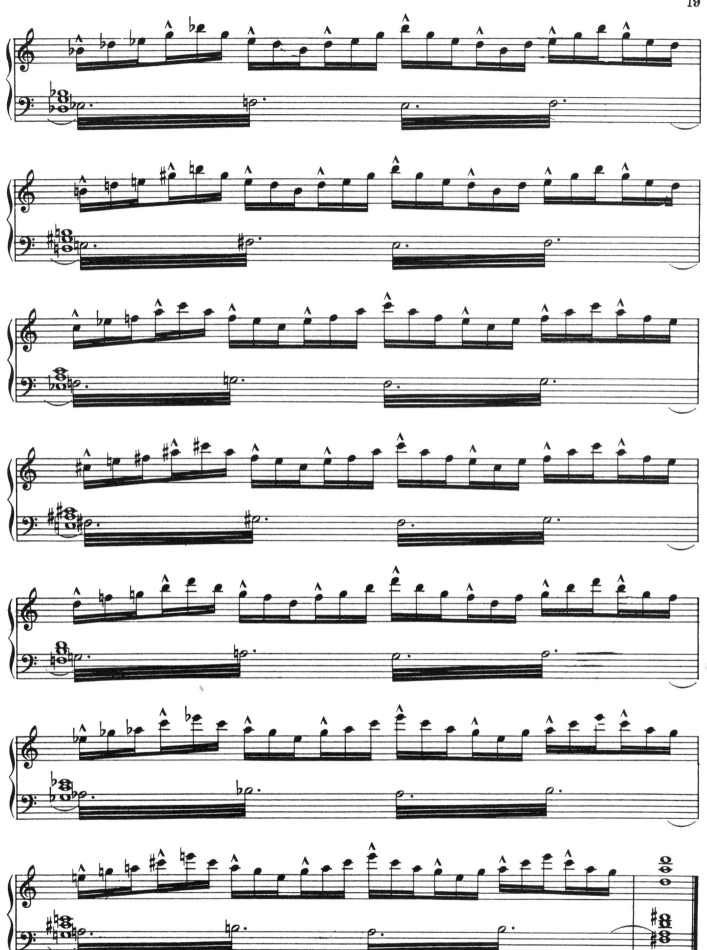

In all keys.

Preparatory Exercises to No. 11.
Practise in all keys.

Preparatory Exercises to Nº 12.

Practise in all keys.

Right hand.

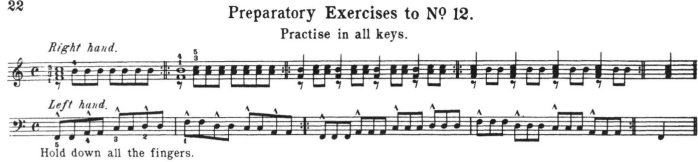

Left hand.

Hold down all the fingers.

Lento.

12.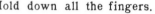

Hold down all the fingers.

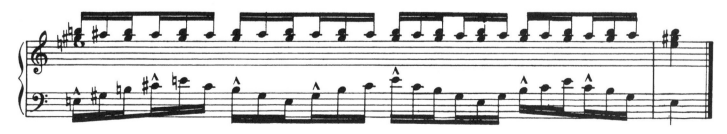

Preparatory Exercises to N⁰ 13.

Practise in all keys.

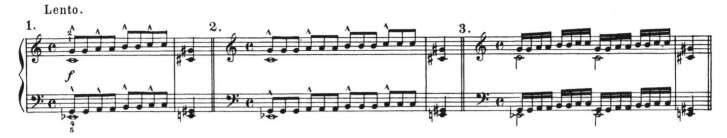

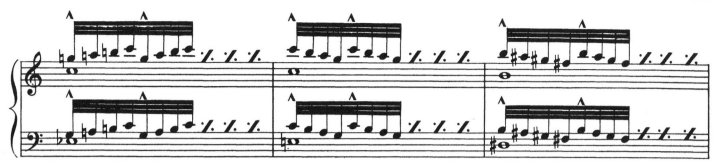

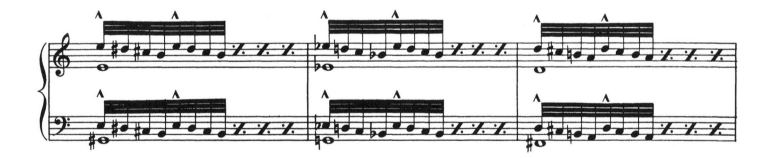

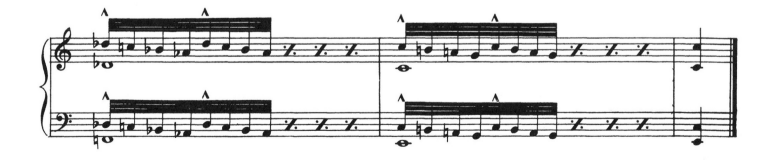

Preparatory Exercises to Nº 14.

Practise in all keys.

Right hand.

Left hand.

Vivace.

14.

legato

15.ª

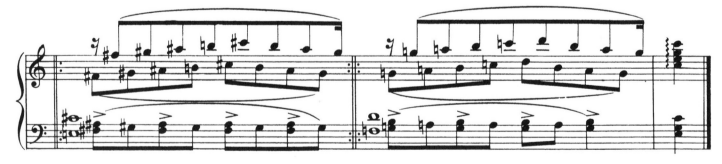

15.ᵇ

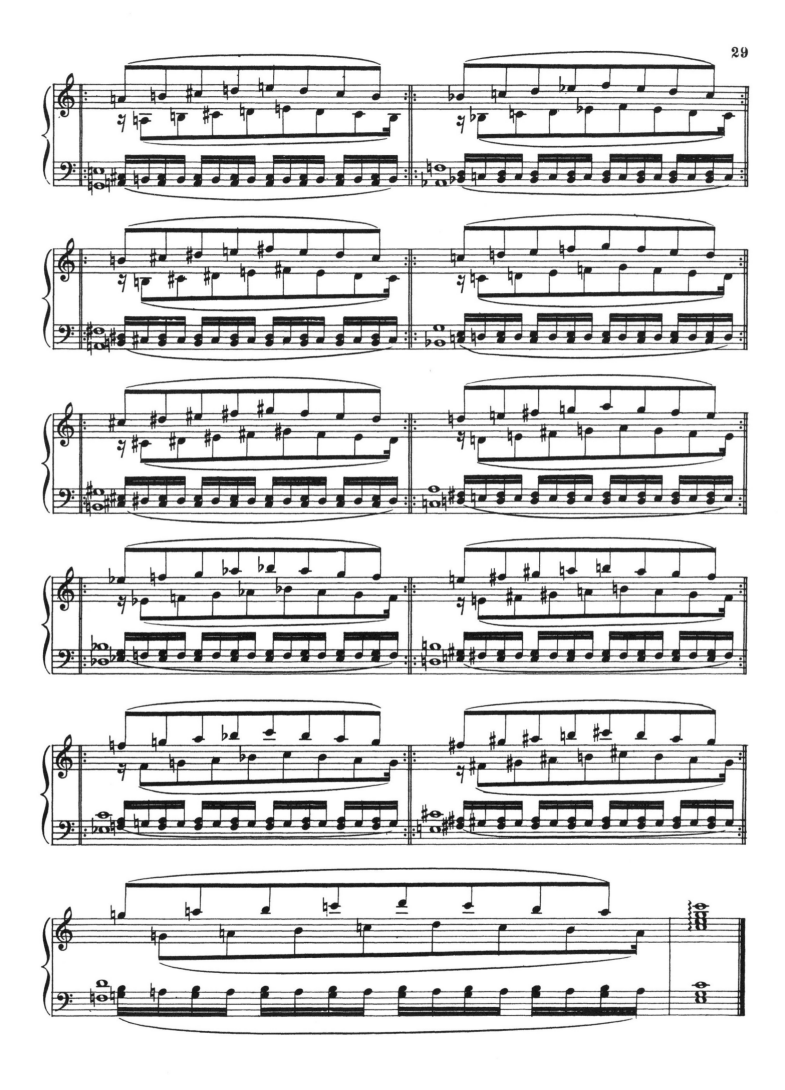

Preparatory Exercises to № 16ª

Practise in all keys.

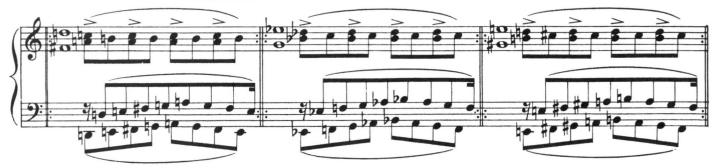

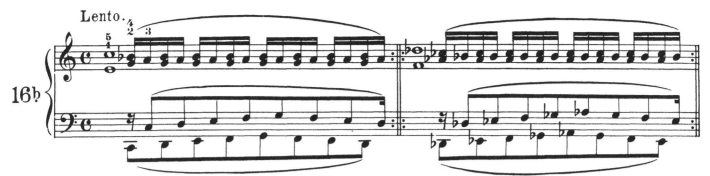

Preparatory Exercises to № 19.

Practise in all keys.

20ͣ Veloce.

20ᵇ Veloce.

8 times.

Preparatory Exercises to № 21.
Practise in all keys.

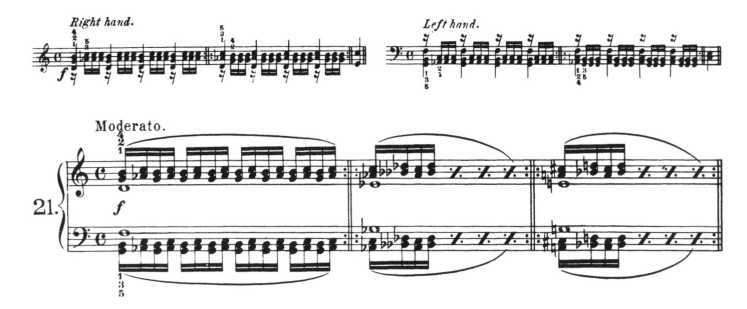

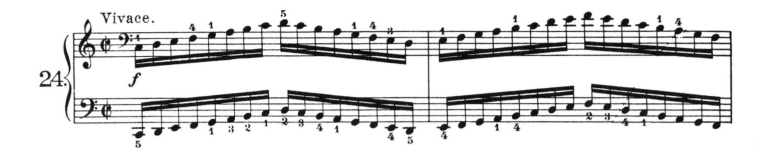

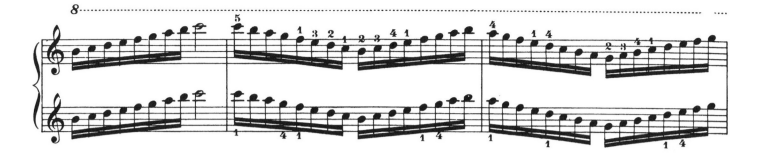

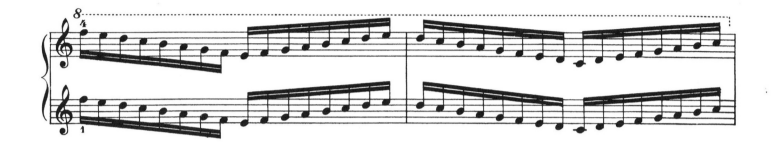

4 times.

25.

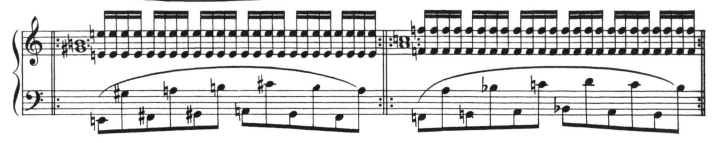

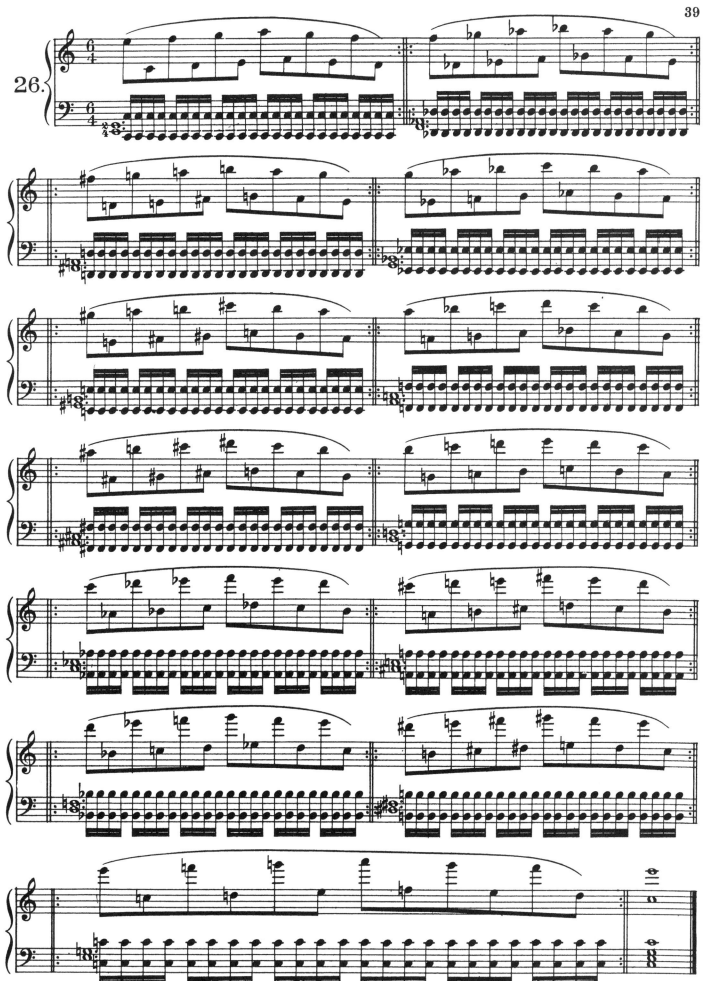

Preparatory Exercises to № 27.

Practise in all keys.

1. Allegro.

f legato

2.

f legato

3.

f legato

27. **Allegro.**

f legato

8 times.

Preparatory Exercises to № 28.

Practise in all keys.

1. Veloce.

2.

Veloce.

28.

Preparatory Exercises to № 29.

Practise in all keys.

Preparatory Exercises to № 30.

Practise in all keys.

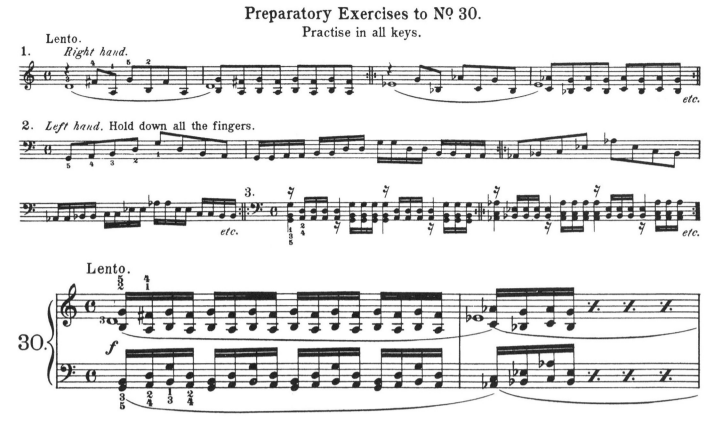

Preparatory Exercises to № 31.

Practise in all keys.

Vivace.

1. *Right hand.* Hold down all the fingers.

etc.

2. *Left hand.*

Vivace.

Hold down all the fingers.

31.

4 times.

45

Preparatory Exercises to № 32.

Practise in all keys.

48

Moderato.
Hold down all the fingers.

33.

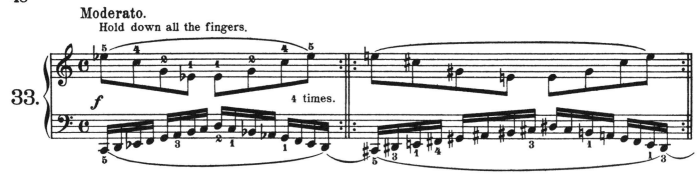

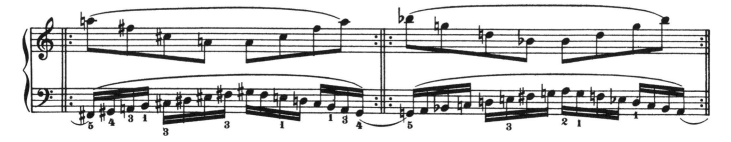

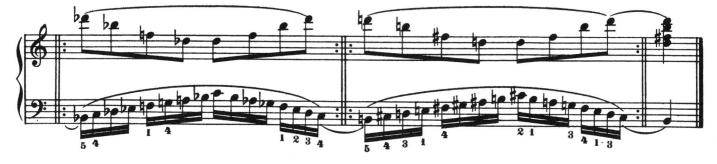

Moderato.

34.

f

4 times.

Hold down all the fingers.

Preparatory Exercises to № 35.

Practise in all keys.

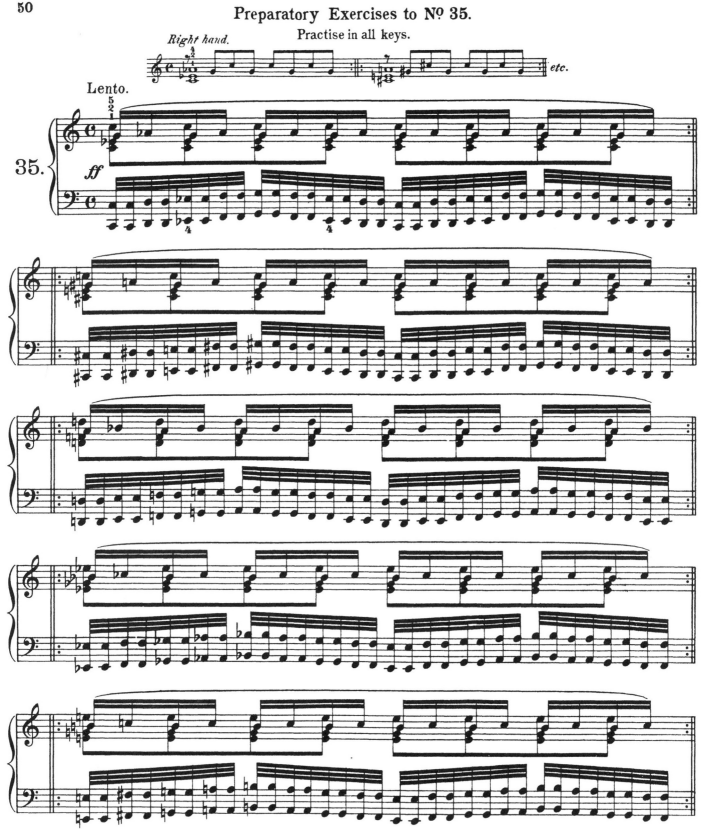

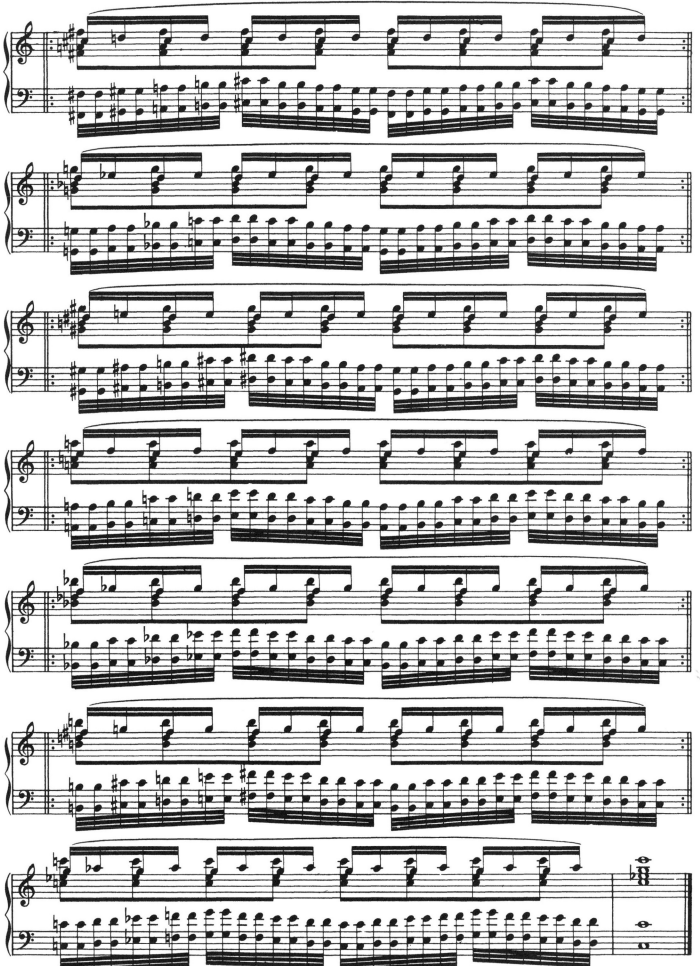

Preparatory Exercises to № 36.

Practise in all keys.

Preparatory Exercises to Nº 37.

Practise in all keys.

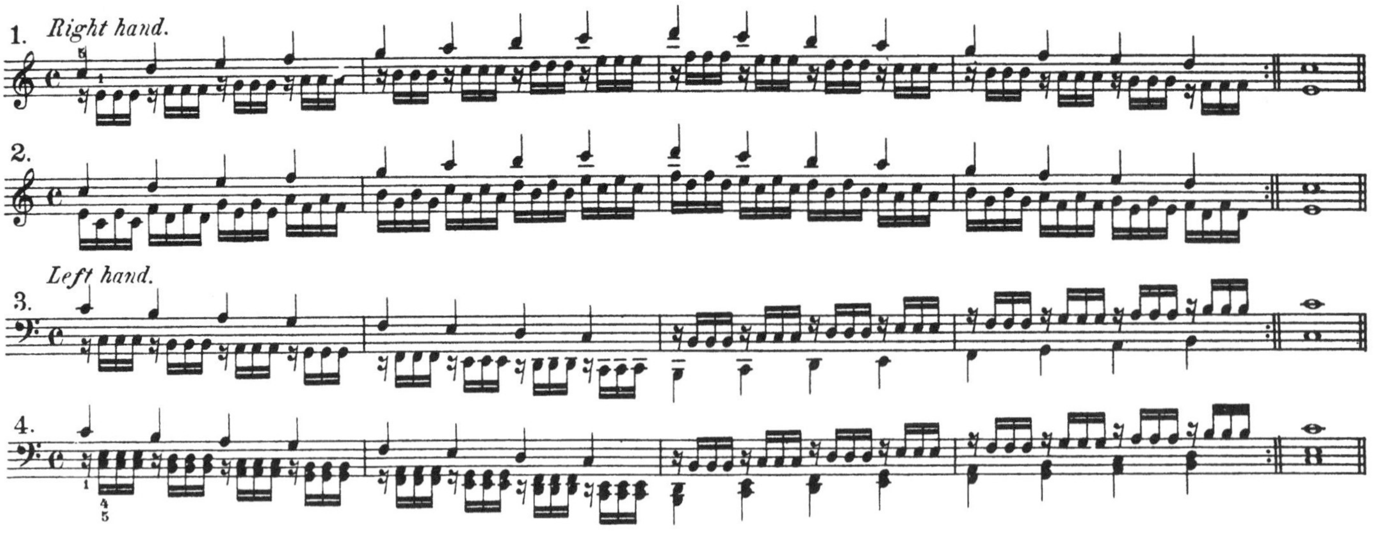

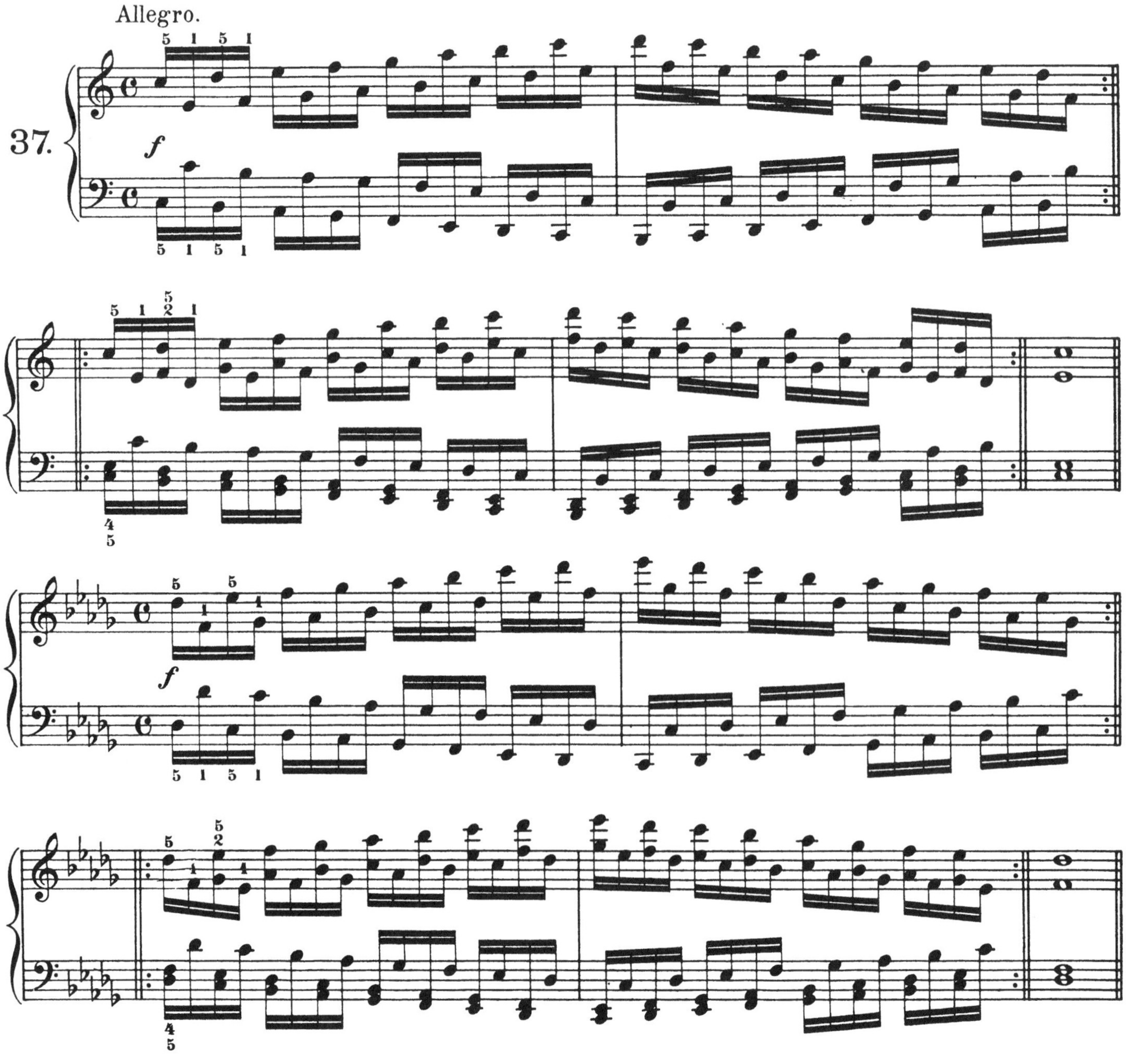

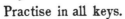

Preparatory Exercises to Nº 38.

Practise in all keys.

Preparatory Exercises to Nº 39.

Practise in all keys.

Right hand.

Left hand.

39.
I.*)

Vivace.

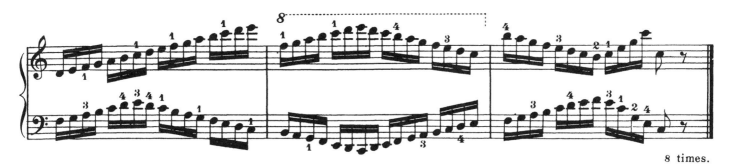

8 times.

*) With the same fingering in *G, D, A* and *E major*.

Vivace.

39.
II.

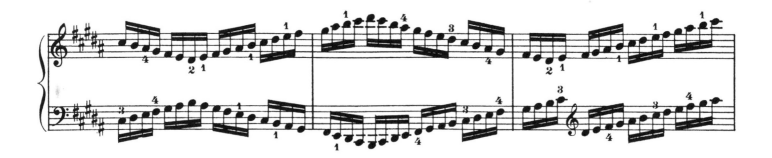

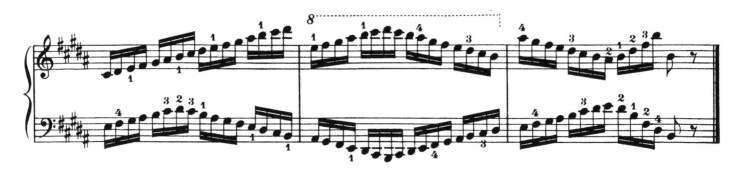

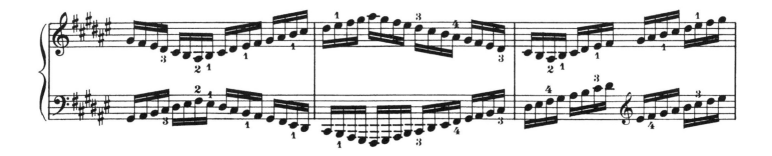

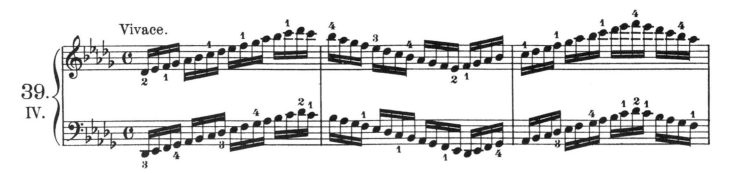

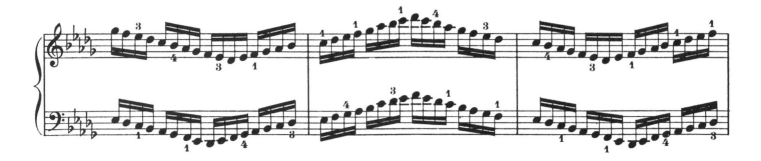

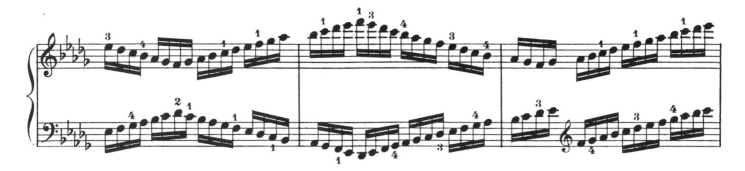

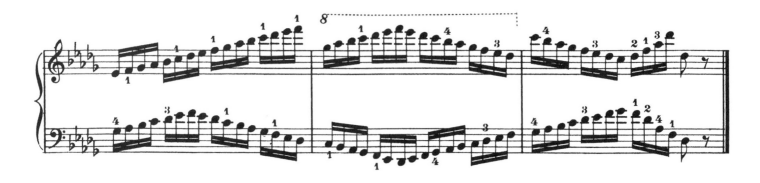

39.
V.

Vivace.

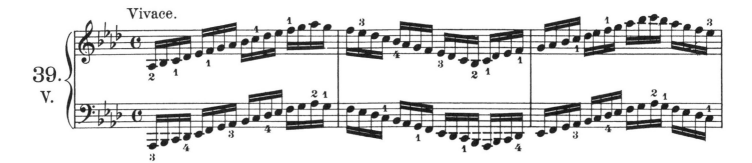

Vivace.

39.
VI.

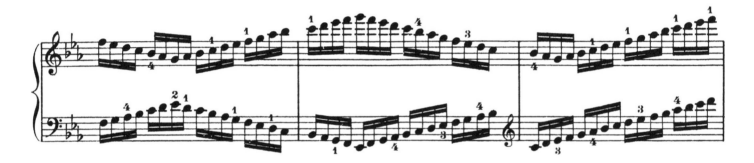

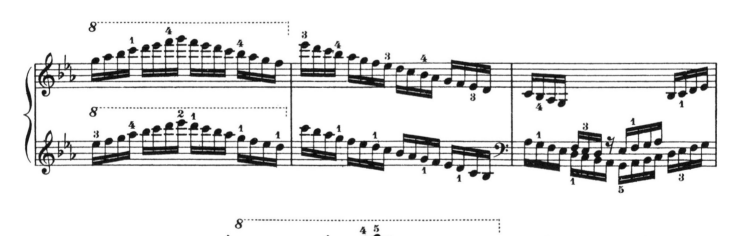

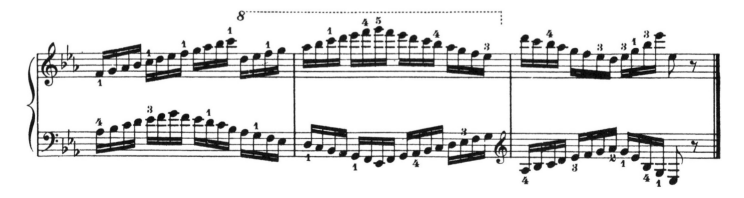

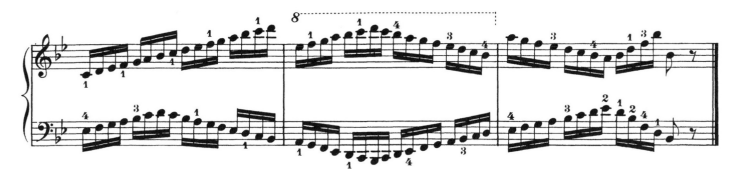

66

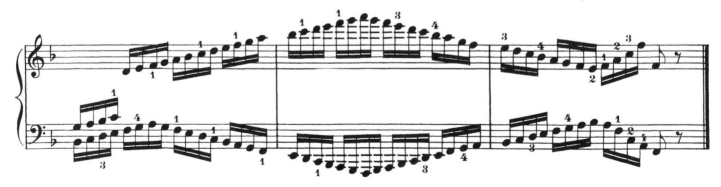

Preparatory Exercises to № 40.

Practise in all keys.

Right hand.

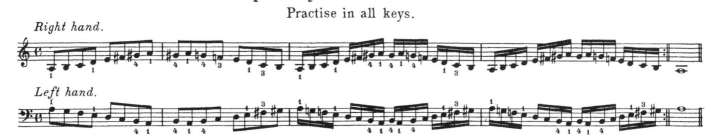

Left hand.

40. I.*) Vivace.

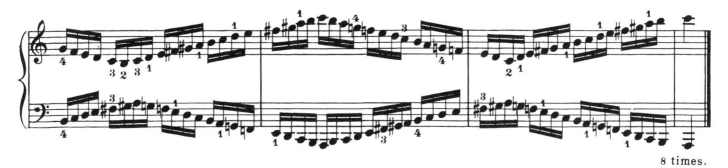

8 times.

* With the same fingering in *E, C, G* and *D minor*.

40.
II.

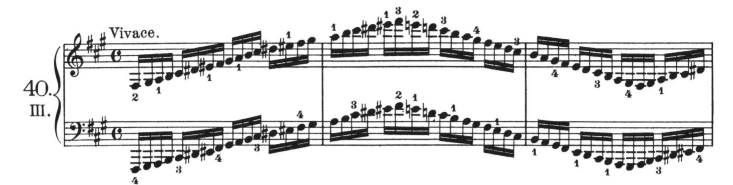

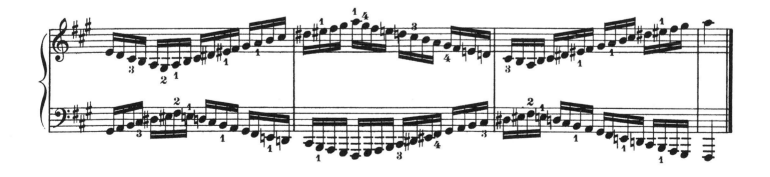

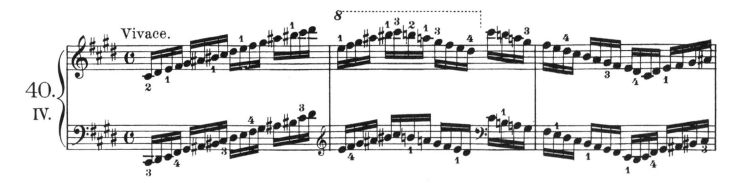

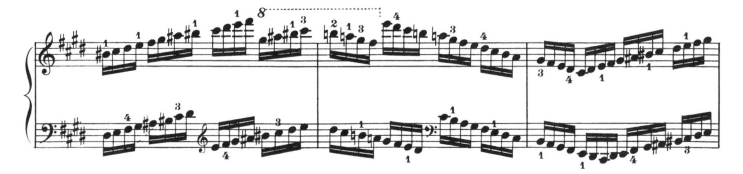

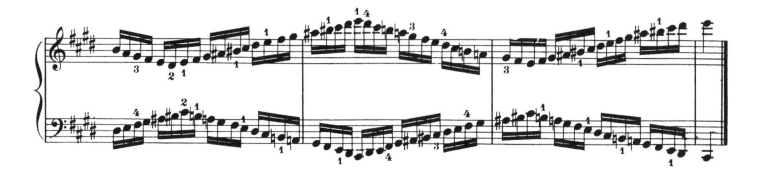

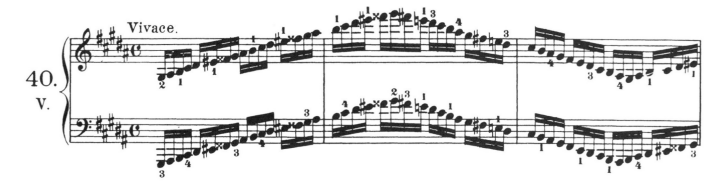

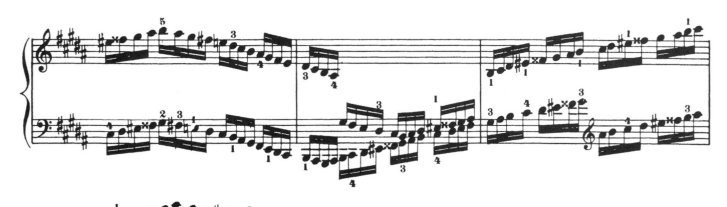

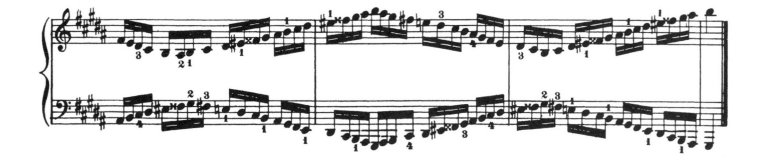

Vivace.

40.
VI.

Vivace.

40.
VII.

Preparatory Exercises to Nº 41.

Practise in all keys.

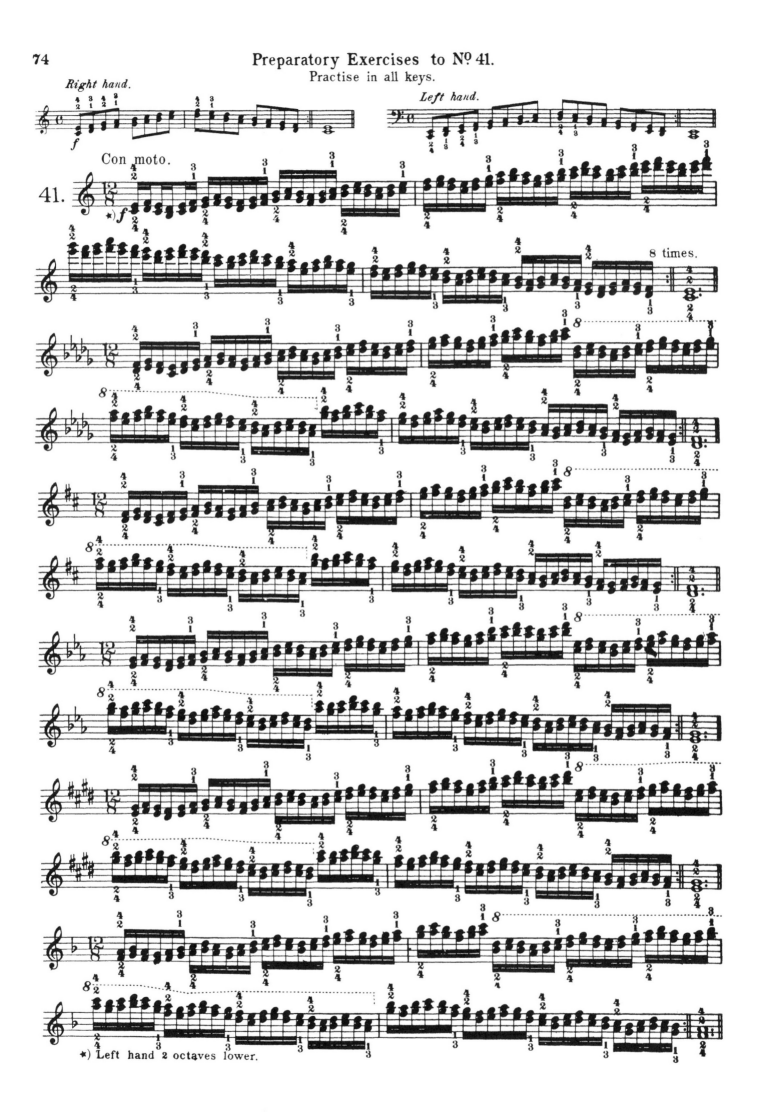

*) Left hand 2 octaves lower.

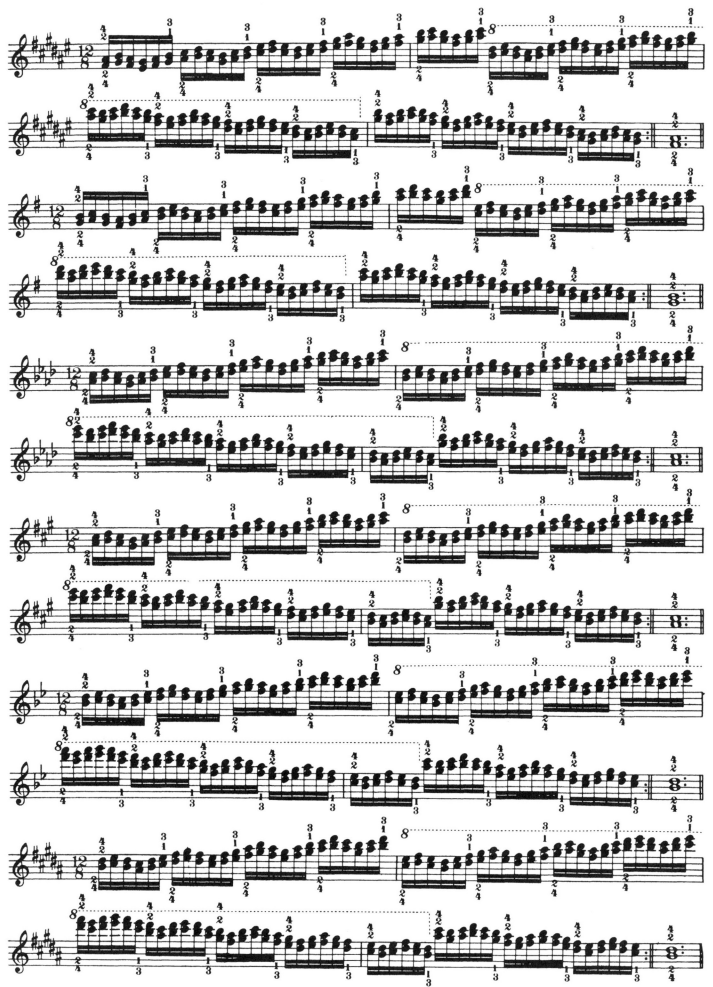

Preparatory Exercises to No. 42.

Practise in all keys.

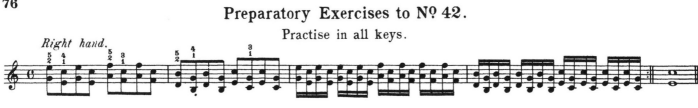

Con moto.

42.

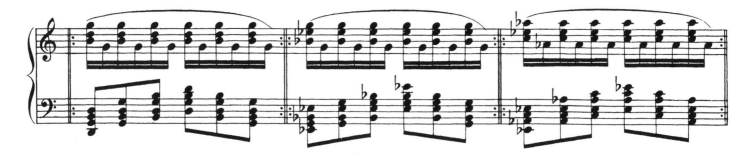

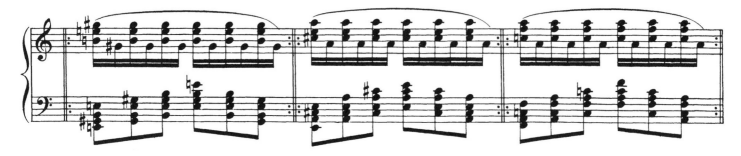

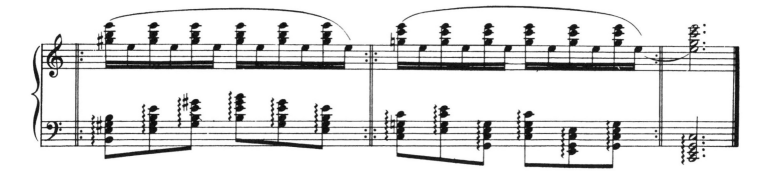

Preparatory Exercises to № 43.

Practise in all keys.

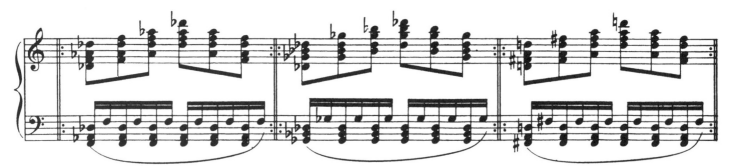

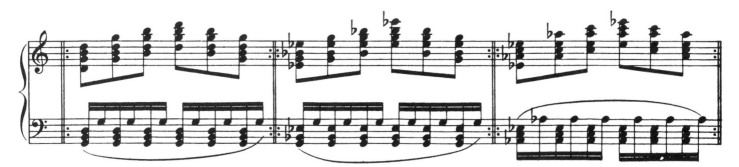

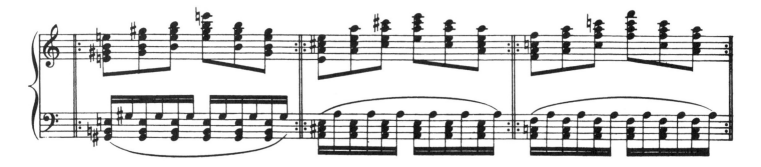

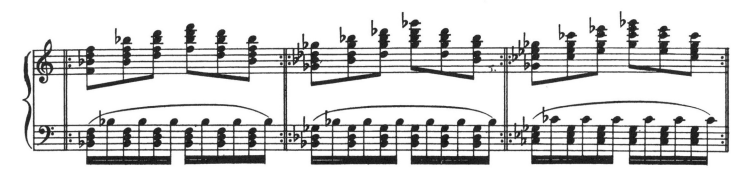

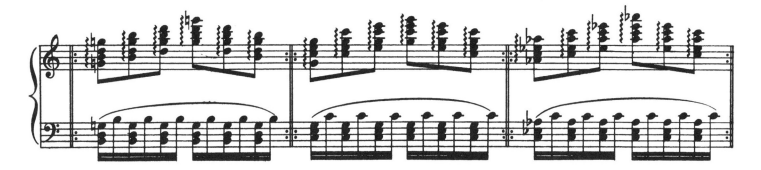

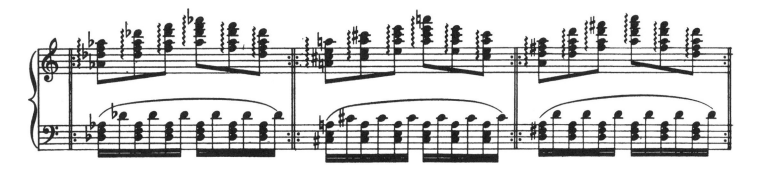

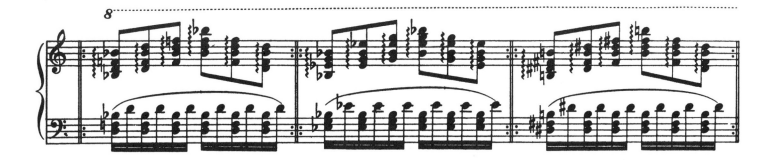

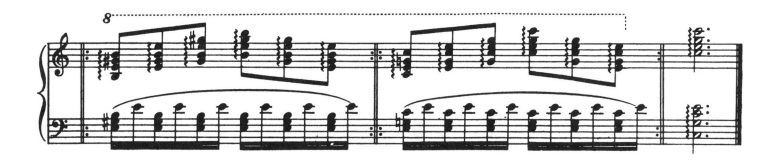

Preparatory Exercises to № 44.

Practise in all keys.

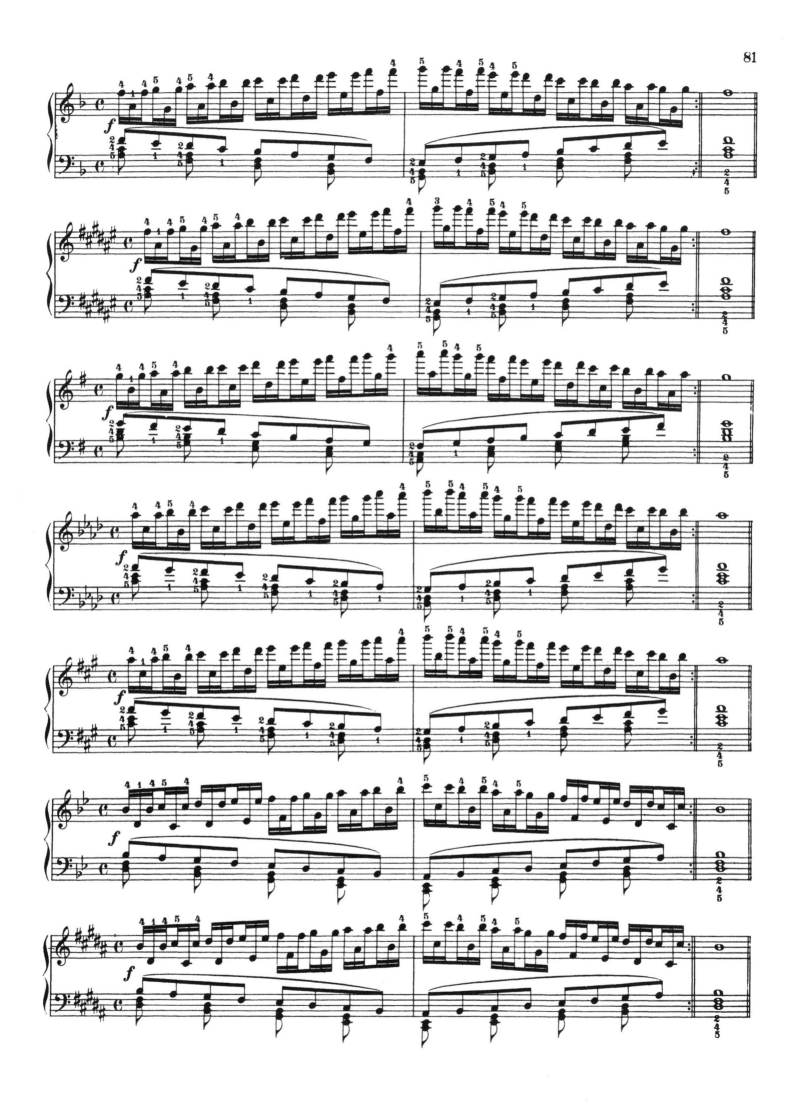

Preparatory Exercises to Nº 45.

Practise in all keys.

Preparatory Exercises to N.º.ˢ 46 and 47.

Practise in all keys.

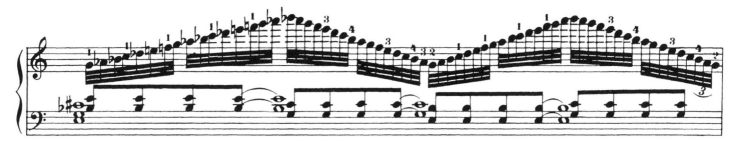

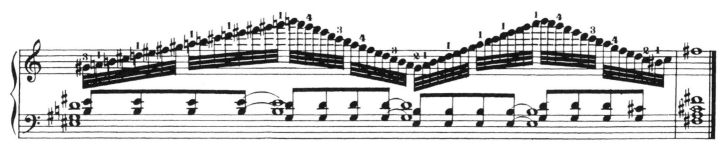

Con moto.

47.

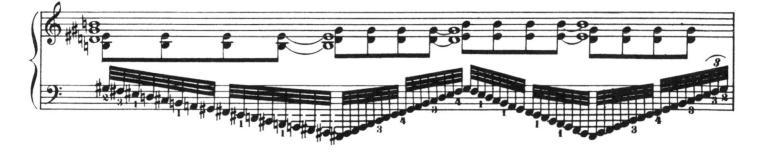

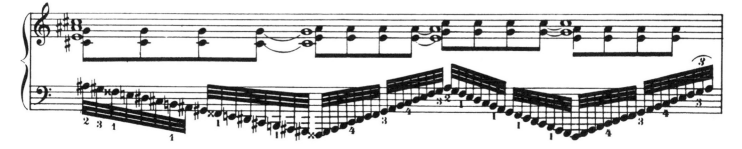

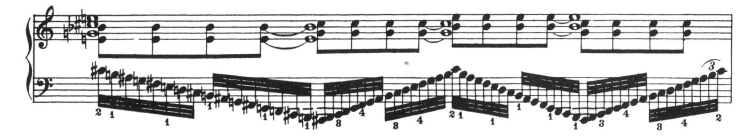

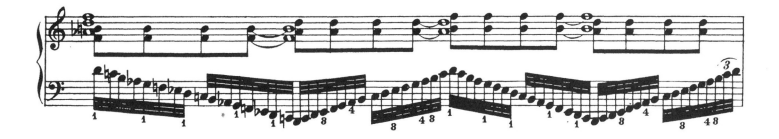

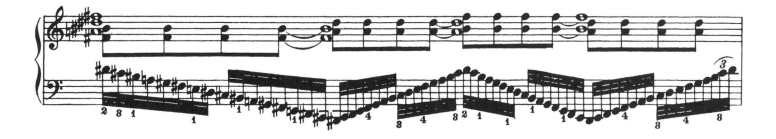

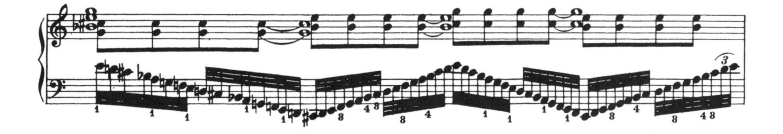

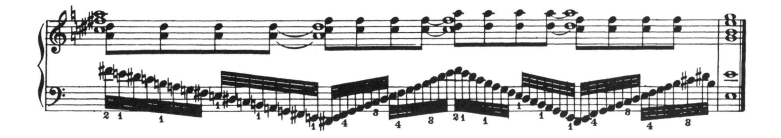

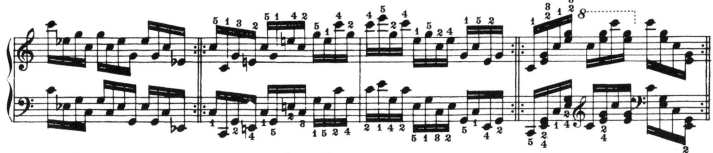

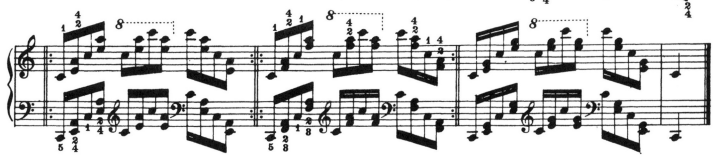

Lento.

52.

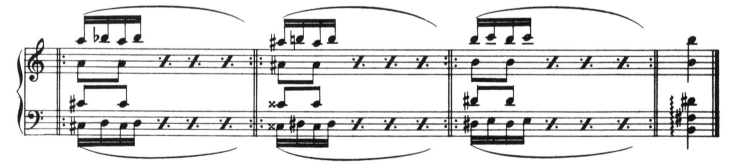

Preparatory Exercises to № 53.

Practise in all keys.

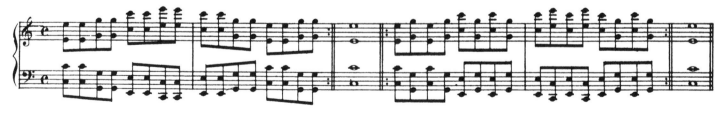

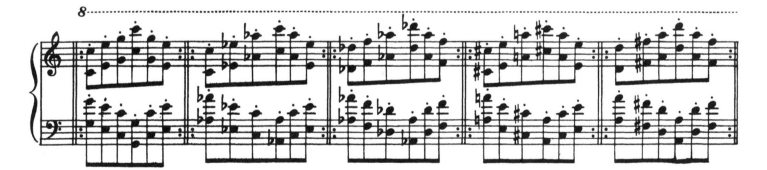

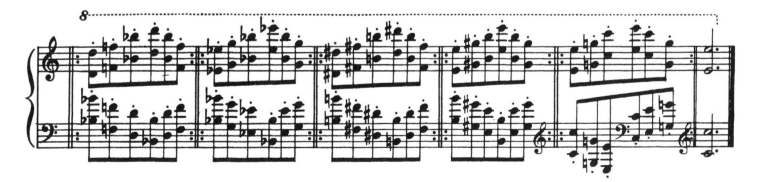

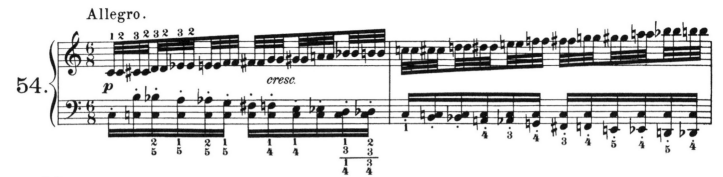

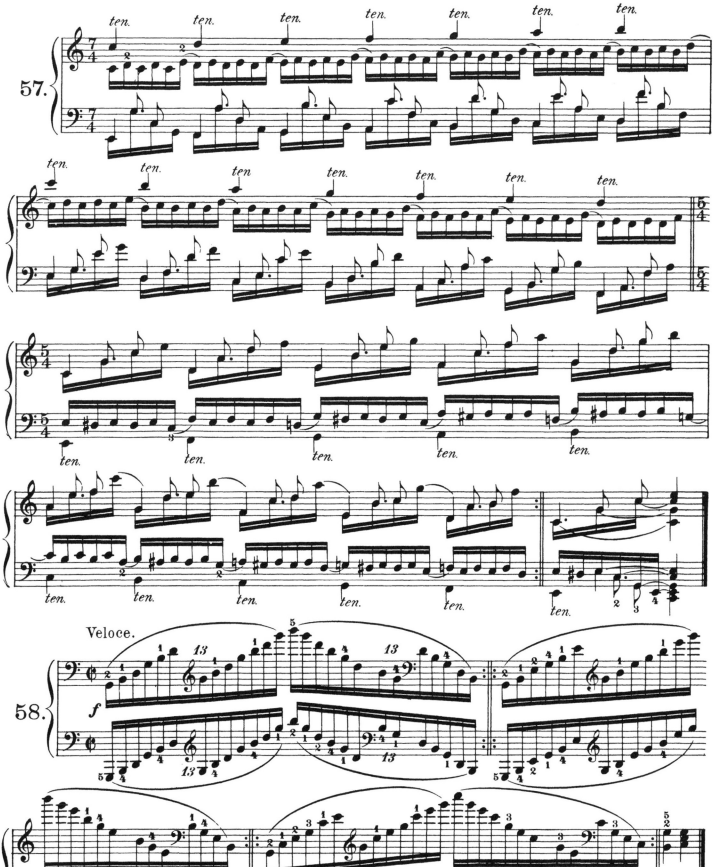

Moderato.

59.

f legato

Preparatory Exercises to № 60.

H. Riemann.

1.

2.

3.

4.

5.

6.

7.

8.

Allegro.

60.

p legato

cresc.

p

Scales in Thirds.

Fingering acc. to Liszt-Tausig.*)

H. Riemann.

*) The fingering of Chopin (Étude Op. 25, № 6, in G♯ minor) does not lead to the highest degree of precision:

N.B.   N.B.   N.B.   N.B.

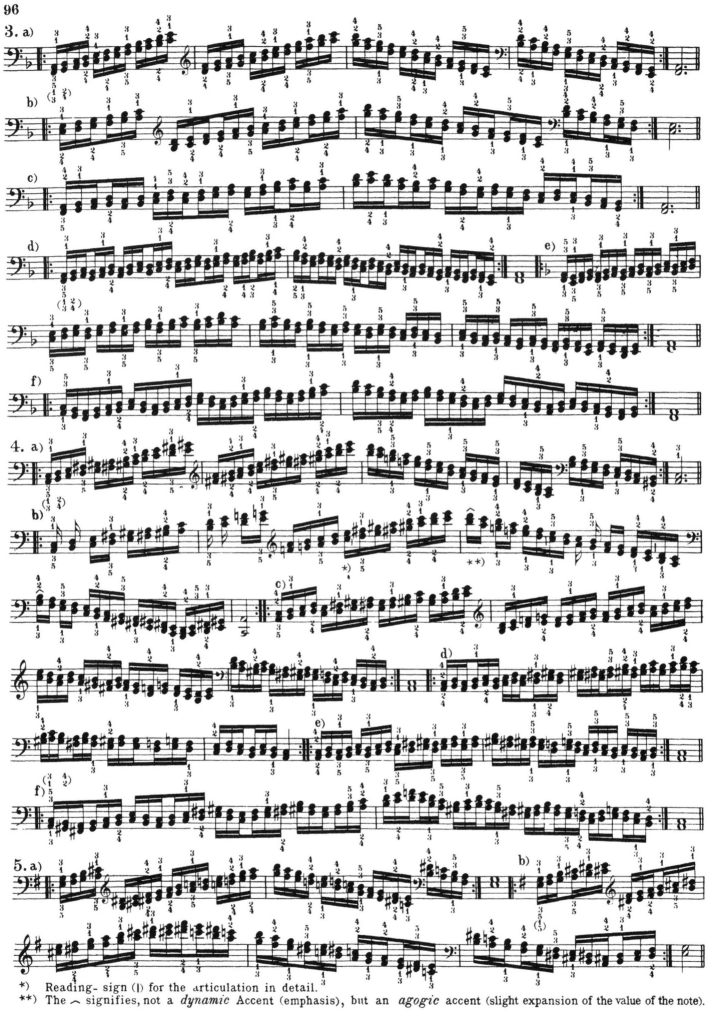

*) Reading- sign (|) for the articulation in detail.
**) The ⌢ signifies, not a *dynamic* Accent (emphasis), but an *agogic* accent (slight expansion of the value of the note).

99